KU-444-967

POPE FRANCIS
IN
IRELAND

Homilies, Speeches and Addresses
of His Holiness

VERITAS

Published 2018 by Veritas Publications
7–8 Lower Abbey Street
Dublin 1, Ireland
publications@veritas.ie
www.veritas.ie

ISBN 978 1 84730 874 0

Copyright © Libreria Editrice Vaticana, 2018

10 9 8 7 6 5 4 3 2 1

The material in this publication is protected by copyright law. Except as may be
permitted by law, no part of the material may be reproduced (including by storage in a
retrieval system) or transmitted in any form or by any means, adapted, rented or lent
without the written permission of the copyright owners. Applications for permissions
should be addressed to the publisher.

Designed by Heather Costello, Veritas Publications
Printed in the Republic of Ireland by Walsh Colour Print, Kerry

Printed on paper made from the wood pulp of managed forests. For every tree felled, at
least one tree is planted, thereby renewing natural resources.

CONTENTS

President Michael D. Higgins and Mrs Sabina Higgins with
Pope Francis, Áras an Uachtaráin

Pope Francis with Minister Katherine Zappone, Minister for
Children and Youth Affairs, Áras an Uachtaráin

VISIT TO THE PRESIDENT OF IRELAND
Áras an Uachtaráin
Saturday, 25 August 2018

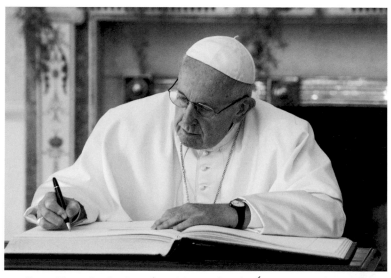

Pope Francis signing the visitors' book, Áras an Uachtaráin

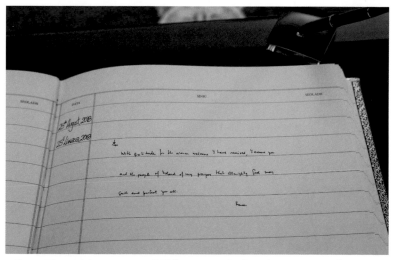

Pope Francis' message: 'With gratitude for the warm welcome I have received, I assure you and the people of Ireland of my prayers that Almighty God may guide and protect you all. Francis.'

Pope Francis with An Taoiseach Leo Varadkar, Dublin Castle

Meeting with Authorities, Civil Society and Diplomatic Corps

ADDRESS OF HIS HOLINESS POPE FRANCIS

Dublin Castle

Saturday, 25 August 2018

Taoiseach, members of government and of the diplomatic corps, ladies and gentlemen,

At the beginning of my visit to Ireland, I am grateful for the invitation to address this distinguished assembly representing the civil, cultural and religious life of the country, together with the members of the diplomatic corps and guests. I appreciate the friendly welcome I have received from the President of Ireland, which reflects the tradition of cordial hospitality for which the Irish are known throughout the world. I likewise appreciate the presence of a delegation from Northern Ireland. I thank the Taoiseach for his words.

As you know, the reason for my visit is to take part in the World Meeting of Families, held this year in Dublin. The Church is, in a real way, a family among families, and senses the need to support families in their efforts to respond faithfully and joyfully to their God-given vocation in society. The Meeting is not only an opportunity for families to reaffirm their commitment to loving fidelity, mutual assistance and reverence for God's gift of life in all its forms, but also to testify to the unique role played by the family in the education of its members and the development of a sound and flourishing social fabric.

Families are the glue of society; their welfare cannot be taken for granted, but must be promoted and protected by every appropriate means

I would like to see the World Meeting of Families as a prophetic witness to the rich patrimony of ethical and spiritual values that it is the duty of every generation to cherish and protect. One need not be a prophet to perceive the difficulties faced by our families in today's rapidly evolving society, or to be troubled by the effects that breakdown in marriage and family life will necessarily entail for the future of our communities at every level. Families are the glue of society; their welfare cannot be taken for granted, but must be promoted and protected by every appropriate means.

It was in the family that each of us took his or her first steps in life. There we learned to live together in harmony, to master our selfish instincts and reconcile our differences, and above all to discern and seek those values that give authentic meaning and fulfilment to our lives. If we speak of our entire world as a single family, it is because we rightly acknowledge the bonds of our common humanity and we sense our call to unity and solidarity, especially with the weakest of our brothers and sisters. Yet all too often, we feel impotent before the persistent evils of racial and ethnic hatred, intractable conflicts and violence, contempt for human dignity and for fundamental human rights, and the growing divide between rich and poor. How much we need to recover, in every instance of political and social life, the sense of being a true family of peoples! And never to lose hope or the courage to persevere in the moral imperative to be peacemakers, reconcilers and guardians of one another.

Here in Ireland, this challenge has a special resonance, in light of the long conflict that separated brothers and sisters of a single family. Twenty years ago, the international community followed attentively the events in Northern Ireland that led to the signing of the Good Friday Agreement. The Irish government, in union with the political, religious and civil leaders of Northern Ireland and the British government, and with the support of other world leaders, created a dynamic context for the peaceful settlement of a conflict that had caused untold pain on both sides. We can give thanks for the two decades of peace that followed this historic agreement, while expressing firm hope that the peace process will overcome every remaining obstacle and help give birth to a future of harmony, reconciliation and mutual trust.

The Gospel reminds us that true peace is ultimately God's gift; it flows from a healed and reconciled heart and branches out to embrace the entire world. Yet it also requires constant conversion on our part, as the source of those spiritual resources needed to build a society of authentic solidarity, justice and service of the common good. Without that spiritual foundation, our ideal of a global family of nations risks becoming no more than another empty platitude. Can we say that the goal of creating economic or financial prosperity leads of itself to a more just and equitable social order? Or could it be that the growth of a materialistic 'throw-away culture' has in fact made us increasingly indifferent to the

> The Gospel reminds us that
> true peace is ultimately God's
> gift; it flows from a healed and
> reconciled heart and branches
> out to embrace the entire world

Pope Francis and An Taoiseach Leo Varadkar, Dublin Castle

poor and to the most defenceless members of our human family, including the unborn, deprived of the very right to life? Perhaps the most disturbing challenges to our consciences in these days is the massive refugee crisis, which will not go away, and whose solution calls for a wisdom, a breadth of vision and a humanitarian concern that go far beyond short-term political decisions.

I am very conscious of the circumstances of our most vulnerable brothers and sisters – I think especially of those women and children who in the past endured particularly difficult situations, and to the orphans of that time. With regard to the most vulnerable, I cannot fail to acknowledge the grave scandal caused in Ireland by the abuse of young people by members of the Church charged with responsibility for their protection and education. I was deeply moved by the words spoken to me by the Minister for Children and Youth Affairs; I thank her for those words. The failure of ecclesiastical authorities – bishops, religious superiors, priests and others – to adequately address these repellent crimes has rightly given rise to outrage and remains a source of pain and shame for the Catholic community. I myself share those sentiments. My predecessor, Pope Benedict, spared no words in recognising both the gravity of the situation and in demanding that 'truly evangelical, just and effective' measures be taken in response to this betrayal of trust (cf. *Pastoral Letter to the Catholics of Ireland*, 10). His frank and decisive intervention continues to serve as an incentive for the efforts of the Church's leadership both to remedy past mistakes and to adopt stringent norms meant to ensure that they do not happen again. More recently, in a Letter to the People of God, I reaffirmed the commitment, and the need for an even greater commitment, to eliminating this scourge in the Church, at any cost.

Each child is, in fact, a precious gift of God, to be cherished, encouraged to develop his or her gifts, and guided to spiritual maturity and human flourishing. The Church in Ireland, past and present, has played a role in promoting the welfare of children that cannot be obscured. It is my hope that the gravity of the abuse scandals, which have cast light on the failings of many, will serve to emphasise the importance of the protection of minors and vulnerable adults on the part of society as a whole. In this regard, all of us are aware of how urgent it is to provide our young people with wise guidance and sound values on their journey to maturity.

Dear friends,

Almost ninety years ago, the Holy See was among the first international institutions to recognise the Irish Free State. That initiative signalled the beginning of many years of dynamic cooperation and harmony, with only an occasional cloud on the horizon. Recently, intensive endeavour and goodwill on both sides have contributed significantly to a promising renewal of those friendly relations for the mutual benefit of all.

The threads of that history reach back to over a millennium and a half ago when the Christian message, preached by Palladius and Patrick, found a home in Ireland and became an integral part of Irish life and culture. Many 'saints and scholars' were inspired to leave these shores and bring their newfound faith to other lands. To this day, the names of Columba, Columbanus, Brigid, Gall, Killian, Brendan and so many others are still revered throughout Europe and beyond. On this island monasticism, as a source of civilisation and artistic creativity, wrote a splendid page in Irish and universal history.

On this island monasticism, as a source of civilisation and artistic creativity, wrote a splendid page in Irish and universal history

Today, as in the past, the men and women who live in this country strive to enrich the life of the nation with the wisdom born of their faith. Even in Ireland's darkest hours, they found in that faith a source of the courage and commitment needed to forge a future of freedom and dignity, justice and solidarity. The Christian message has been an integral part of that experience, and has shaped the language, thought and culture of people on this island.

It is my prayer that Ireland, in listening to the polyphony of contemporary political and social discussion, will not be forgetful of the powerful strains of the Christian message that have sustained it in the past, and can continue to do so in the future.

With these thoughts, I cordially invoke upon you, and upon all the beloved Irish people, God's blessings of wisdom, joy and peace. Thank you.

Pope Francis and Archbishop Diarmuid Martin
at Saint Mary's Pro-Cathedral

Visit to Saint Mary's Pro-Cathedral

ADDRESS OF THE HOLY FATHER FRANCIS

Saint Mary's Pro-Cathedral (Dublin)

Saturday, 25 August 2018

Good afternoon!

Dear friends,

I am pleased that we can meet in this historic Pro-Cathedral of Saint Mary's, which has seen countless celebrations of the sacrament of matrimony over the years. Looking out at you, at your youth, I ask myself: so then it isn't true what everybody says, that young people don't want to get married! Thank you. Getting married and sharing one's life is something beautiful. We have a saying in Spanish: 'Sorrow shared by two is half a sorrow; joy shared by two is joy and a half.' That is what marriage is like.

How much love has been expressed here, and how many graces have been received in this holy place! I thank Archbishop Martin for his cordial welcome. I am especially happy to be with all of you, engaged couples and married couples at different stages on the journey of sacramental love. It is also nice to hear the beautiful music coming from over there ... the sound of babies crying! That is a sign of hope, the loveliest music, but it is also the best sermon, to hear a baby crying, because it is a cry of hope, [a sign] that life goes on, that life goes forward, that love is fruitful. Look at the babies ... But I greeted an elderly person too: we also have to look at the elderly, because the elderly are full of wisdom. Listen to what the elderly have to say, [ask them] 'What was your life like?'

The world needs a revolution of love. Let that revolution begin with you and your families!

I liked the fact that you [turning to Vincent and Teresa, the elderly couple who were the first to speak] spoke first, after fifty years of marriage, because you have so much experience to share. The future and the past meet in the present. They – let me use the word – the 'old', have wisdom. Even mothers-in-law have wisdom! [laughter] And children must listen to their wisdom, you young people ought to listen to their wisdom, and talk to them in order to keep going, because they are your roots. They are the roots and you draw from those roots in order to keep moving forward. I am going to come back to this later on, for sure, but I want to say it now, from the heart.

As I mentioned, I am particularly grateful for the testimony of Vincent and Teresa, who spoke to us of their experience of fifty years of marriage and family life. Thank you both for your words of encouragement and challenge addressed to a new generation of newlyweds and engaged couples, not only here in Ireland but throughout the world. They are not going to be like you; they are different. But they need your experience to be different, to keep moving forward. It is so important to listen to the elderly, to our grandparents! We have much to learn from your experience of a married life sustained daily by the grace of the sacrament.

I want to ask you: did you quarrel a lot? But that is part of marriage! A marriage without arguments is pretty boring … [laughter]. Yet there is a secret: plates can even fly, but the secret is to make up before the end of the day. And to make up there is no need to talk; a caress is enough, like that, and peace returns. Do you know why this is important? Because if you do not make up before going to bed, the 'cold war' of the following day is too dangerous, resentment builds up ... Yes, fight all you want, but make up at night. All right? Don't forget this, you young people ...

In growing together in this 'partnership of life and love', you have experienced many joys and, to be sure, not a few sorrows as well. Together with all spouses who have come far along this path, you are the keepers of our collective memory. We will always need your faith-filled witness. It is a precious resource for young couples, who look to the future with excitement and hope and, perhaps ... a touch of trepidation: what will that future be like?

I also thank the young couples who have asked me several forthright questions. They are not easy to answer! Denis and Sinead are about to embark on a journey of love that, in God's plan, entails a lifelong commitment. They asked how they can help others to see that marriage is not simply an institution but a vocation, a life that moves forward, a conscious and lifelong decision to cherish, assist and protect one another.

Surely we have to acknowledge that nowadays we are not used to anything that really lasts for the whole of our lives. We are living in a 'culture of the provisional', we are used to it. If I feel hungry or thirsty, I can eat; but my feeling of being full does not last even a day. If I have a job, I know that I might lose it against my will, or I may have to choose a different career. It is even hard to keep track of the world as it changes all around us, as people come and go in our lives, as promises are made but often broken or left unfulfilled. Perhaps what you are really asking me is something even more basic: Is there *anything* precious that endures at all? This is the question. It seems that nothing beautiful or precious lasts. 'Isn't there anything precious that lasts? Even love itself?'

Pope Francis departs Saint Mary's Pro-Cathedral

Jesus' love is, for couples, a rock
and refuge in times of trial, but more
importantly, a source of constant
growth in pure and enduring love

There is a temptation that the phrase 'all the days of my life' that you will say to one another may change and, in time, die. If love does not grow by more love, it doesn't last long. Those words 'all the days of my life' are a commitment to make love grow, because love has nothing of the provisional. Call it excitement, call it, I don't know, enchantment, but real love is definitive, a 'you and I'. As we say in my country, it is 'half of the orange': you are my half of the orange and I am your half of the orange. That is what love is like: everything and every day for all the days of your life. It is easy to find ourselves caught up in the culture of the provisional, the ephemeral, and that culture strikes at the very roots of our processes of maturation, our growth in hope and love. How can we experience 'what truly lasts' in this culture of the ephemeral? This is a tough question: how can we experience, in this culture of the ephemeral, what is truly lasting?

Here is what I would say to you. Of all the kinds of human fruitfulness, marriage is unique. It is about a love that gives rise to new life. It involves mutual responsibility for the transmission of God's gift of life, and it provides a stable environment in which that new life can grow and flourish. Marriage in the Church, that is, the sacrament of matrimony, shares in a special way in the mystery of God's eternal love. When a Christian man and woman enter the bond of marriage, God's grace enables them freely to promise one another an exclusive and enduring love. Their union thus becomes a sacramental sign – this is important – the sacrament of marriage becomes a sacramental sign of the new and eternal covenant between the Lord and his bride, the Church. Jesus is ever present in their midst. He sustains them throughout life in their mutual gift of self, in fidelity and in indissoluble unity (cf. *Gaudium et Spes*, 48). Jesus' love is, for couples, a rock and refuge in times of trial, but more importantly, a source of constant growth in pure and enduring love. Gamble big, for your entire life! Take a risk!

Because marriage is also a risk, but it is a risk worth taking. For your whole life, because that is how love is.

We know that love is God's dream for us and for the whole human family. Please, never forget this! God has a dream for us and he asks us to make it our own. So do not be afraid of that dream! Dream big! Cherish that dream and dream it together each day anew. In this way, you will be able to support one another with hope, strength and forgiveness at those moments when the path grows rocky and it becomes hard to see the road ahead. In the Bible, God binds himself to remain faithful to his covenant, even when we grieve him or grow weak in our love. What does God say in the Bible to his people? Listen carefully: 'I will never fail you nor forsake you!' (Heb 13:5). And you, as husbands and wives, anoint one another with those words of promise, every day for the rest of your lives. And never stop dreaming! Keep repeating in your heart: 'I will never fail you or forsake you!'

Stephen and Jordan are newlyweds and they asked the very important question of how parents can pass the faith on to their children. I know that the Church here in Ireland has carefully prepared catechism programmes for teaching the faith in schools and parishes. This is, of course, essential. Yet the first and most important place for passing on the faith is *the home*. It is in the home that we learn to believe, through the quiet daily example of parents who love our Lord and trust in his word. There, in the home, which we can call the 'domestic church', children learn the meaning of fidelity, integrity and sacrifice. They see how their mother and father interact with each other, how they care for each other and for others, how they love God and love the Church. In this way, children can breathe in the fresh air of the Gospel and learn to understand, judge and act in a manner worthy of the legacy of faith they have received. The faith, brothers and sisters, is passed on 'around the family table', at home in ordinary conversation, in the language that persevering love alone knows how to speak.

Never forget this, brothers and sisters: faith is passed on in everyday speech! The speech of the home, everyday life, life in the family. Think of the seven Maccabee brothers, how their mother spoke to them 'in everyday speech', the language in which they first learned about God. It is more difficult to receive the faith – it can be done, but it is more difficult – if it has not been received in your native language, at home, in everyday speech. I am tempted to mention an experience I had as a child … If it helps, I'll tell you. I remember once – I was about five years old – I came home and there, in the dining room, I saw my mother and my father (who had come home from work just before me) kissing. I will never forget it! How beautiful! Though weary from work, he had the strength to express his love for his wife. May your children see you do the same, caressing one another, kissing one another, embracing one another. This is magnificent, because that is how they learn the everyday speech of love, and faith. This everyday speech of love.

So it is important to pray together as a family; speak of good and holy things, and let our Mother Mary into your life and the life of your family. Celebrate the feasts of the Christian people; let your children see what it is to celebrate a family feast. Live in deep solidarity with those who suffer and are at the edges of society, and let your children learn to do the same.

The faith, brothers and sisters, is passed on 'around the family table', at home in ordinary conversation, in the language that persevering love alone knows how to speak

Pope Francis at Saint Mary's Pro-Cathedral

Another story. I knew a lady who had three children, about seven, five and three years of age. The couple had a good marriage, they had great faith and they taught their children to help the poor, because they themselves used to help them. Once while they were at lunch, the mother and three children (their father was at work), there was a knock on the door and the oldest one went to answer it. He came back and said: 'Mom, there is a poor person who is asking for something to eat.' They were eating breaded beef – which is very tasty! [laughter] – and the mother asked the children: 'What should we do?' All three replied: 'Mom, give him something!' There were a few slices of beef left over, but the mother took a knife and started to take half of everyone's steak. The children protested: 'No, Mom, give him one of those, not ours!' [The mother replied:] 'No, you give the poor from what you have, not from what is left over!' That is how that faith-filled woman taught her children to give of their own to the poor. All these things can be done at home, when there is love, when there is faith, when everyone speaks the 'everyday speech' of faith. In a word, your children will learn from you how to live a Christian life; you will be their first teachers in the faith, handing on the faith.

The virtues and truths the Lord teaches us are not necessarily popular in today's world – sometimes the Lord asks things that are not popular. Today's world has little use for the weak, the vulnerable and all those it deems 'unproductive'. The world tells us to be strong and independent, with little care for those who are alone or sad, rejected or sick, not yet born or dying. In a moment, I will go privately to meet some families facing grave challenges and real hardship, but who are being shown love and support by the Capuchin Fathers. Our world needs a revolution of love! The tumult of our times is really one of selfishness, of personal interests … The world needs a revolution of love. Let that revolution begin with you and your families!

A few months ago, someone told me that we are losing our ability to love. Slowly but surely, we are forgetting the direct language of a caress, the strength of tenderness. There will be no revolution of love without a revolution of tenderness! It is as if the word 'tenderness' has been taken out of the dictionary. By your example, may your children be guided to become a kinder, more loving, more faith-filled generation, for the renewal of the Church and of all Irish society.

In this way, your love, which is God's gift, will sink ever deeper roots. No family can grow if it forgets its roots. Children will not grow in love if they do not learn how to converse with their grandparents. So let your love sink deep roots! Let us never forget that 'all the blossoms on the tree draw life from what lies buried beneath' (FL Bernárdez, sonnet, *Si para recobrar lo recobrado*). Those are the words of an Argentinian poem, let me give it a little publicity!

Together with the Pope, may the families of the whole Church, represented this afternoon by couples old and young, give thanks to God for the gift of faith and the grace of Christian marriage. In turn, let us promise the Lord that we will serve the coming of his kingdom of holiness, justice and peace by our fidelity to the vows we have made, and by our steadfastness in love!

Thank you for this meeting!

And now I ask you to pray together the Prayer for the Meeting of Families. Then I will give you my blessing. And I ask you to pray for me. Don't forget!

Pope Francis at Saint Mary's Pro-Cathedral

Pope Francis with Br Kevin Crowley and Archbishop Diarmuid Martin,
Capuchin Day Centre, Dublin

Visit to the Capuchin Day Centre for Homeless People

GREETING OF THE HOLY FATHER FRANCIS

Capuchin Day Centre for Homeless People (Dublin)

Saturday, 25 August 2018

Dear brother, dear bishop, dear Capuchin brothers, and all of you, my brothers and sisters!

You [Br Kevin Crowley, the Capuchin brother who welcomed the Holy Father] said that the Capuchins are known as the Brothers of the People, close to the people, and this is true. If at times, some Capuchin community goes distant from the people of God, it falls. You are especially attuned with the people of God, and indeed, with the poor. You have the grace of contemplating the wounds of Jesus in those in need, those who suffer, those who are unfortunate or destitute, or full of vices and defects. For you, this is the flesh of Christ. This is your witness and the Church needs it. Thank you.

One more thing and then [turning to the poor] I will speak to you. Another thing that you said touched my heart. That you don't ask any questions. It is Jesus who comes [in the poor]. You ask no questions. You accept life as it comes, you give comfort and, if need be, you forgive. This makes me think – as a reproof – of those priests who instead live by asking questions about other people's lives and who in confession dig, dig, dig into consciences. Your witness teaches priests to listen, to be close, to forgive and not to ask too many questions. To be simple, as Jesus said that father was when his son returned, full of sins and vices. That father did not

A presentation is made to Pope Francis by Br Kevin Crowley (left) and
Br Sean Donohoe, Capuchin Day Centre, Dublin

sit in a confessional and start asking question after question. He accepted the son's repentance and embraced him. May your witness to the people of God, and this heart capable of forgiving without causing pain, reach all priests. Thank you!

And you, dear brothers and sisters, I thank you for the love and the trust that you have for the Capuchin brothers. Thank you because you come here with trust! Let me say one thing to you. Do you know why you come here with trust? Because they help you without detracting from your dignity. For them, each of you is Jesus Christ. Thank you for the trust that you give us. You are the Church, you are God's people. Jesus is with you. They will give you the things you need, but listen to the advice they give you; they will always give you good advice. And if you have something, some doubt, some hurt, talk to them and they will give you good advice. You know that they love you: otherwise, this Centre would not exist. Thank you for your trust. And one last thing. Pray! Pray for the Church. Pray for priests. Pray for the Capuchins. Pray for the bishops, for your bishop. Pray for me too ... I allow myself to ask all this. Pray for priests, don't forget.

Thank you so much! Now, each of you, think in your heart of all those who are dear to you, because I will also bless them, you and them. And another thing: if any of you has an enemy or anyone you dislike, think of them too, and they will also receive the blessing.

God bless you all, the Father, the Son and the Holy Spirit. Thank you very much.

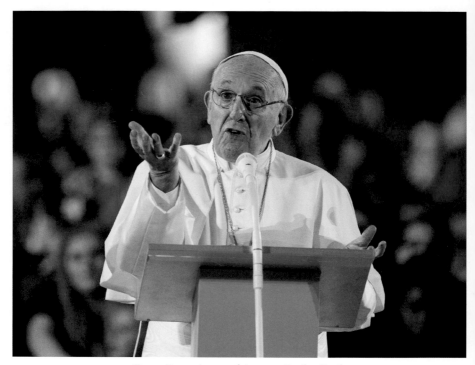

Pope Francis speaking at Croke Park

Feast of Families

ADDRESS OF HIS HOLINESS POPE FRANCIS

Croke Park Stadium (Dublin)

Saturday, 25 August 2018

Dia dhaoibh (Irish for 'good evening!')

Dear brothers and sisters, good evening!

I am grateful to all of you for your warm welcome. It is good to be here! It is good to celebrate, for celebration makes us more human and more Christian. It also helps us to share the joy of knowing that Jesus loves us, he accompanies us on our journey of life, and each day he draws us closer to himself.

In any family celebration, everyone's presence is felt: fathers, mothers, grandparents, grandchildren, uncles and aunts, cousins, those who cannot come and those who live too far away, everyone. Today in Dublin we are gathered for a family celebration of thanksgiving to God for who we are: one family in Christ, spread throughout the world. The Church is the family of God's children. A family in which we rejoice with those who are rejoicing, and weep with those who grieve or feel knocked down by life. A family in which we care for everyone, for God our Father has made all of us his children in Baptism. That is one reason why I keep encouraging parents to baptise their children as soon as possible, so that they can become part of this great family of God. We need to invite everyone to the party, even the smallest child! That is why children should be baptised soon after birth. There is something else: if a child is baptised as a baby, the Holy Spirit enters that child's heart. Let's make a comparison [between]

Pope Francis at the Phoenix Park Mass

a child who is unbaptised, because the parents say: 'No, wait till he or she grows up', and a baby who is baptised and has the Holy Spirit within. That child is stronger, because he or she has the strength of God within!

You, dear families, are the vast majority of the People of God. What would the Church look like without you? A church of statues, a church of lone individuals ... It was to help us recognise the beauty and importance of the family, with its lights and shadows, that the exhortation *Amoris Laetitia* on the joy of love was written, and that I wanted the theme of this World Meeting of Families to be 'The Gospel of the Family, Joy for the World'. God wants every family to be a beacon of the joy of his love in our world. What does this mean? It means that we, who have encountered God's saving love, try, with or without words, to express it in little acts of kindness in our daily routine and in the most hidden moments of our day.

And what is this called? It is called *holiness*. I like to speak of the saints 'next door', all those ordinary people who reflect God's presence in the life and history of our world (cf. *Gaudete et Exsultate*, 6–7). The vocation to love and to holiness is not something reserved for a privileged few. No. Even now, if we have eyes to see, we can see it being lived out all around us. It is silently present in the heart of all those families that offer love, forgiveness and mercy when they see the need, and do so quietly, without great fanfare. The Gospel of the family is truly joy for the world, since there, in our families, Jesus can always be found, dwelling in simplicity and poverty as he did in the home of the Holy Family of Nazareth.

Christian marriage and family life are only seen in all their beauty and attractiveness if they are anchored in the love of God, who created us in his own image, so that we might give him glory as icons of his love and holiness in the world.

> Small and simple acts of forgiveness, renewed each day, are the foundation upon which a solid Christian family life is built

Fathers and mothers, grandfathers and grandmothers, children and grandchildren: each and every one of us. All of us are called to find, in the family, our fulfilment in love. God's grace helps us daily to live as one in mind and heart. Even daughters-in-law and mothers-in-law! No one said this would be easy. You know that better than I. It is like making tea: it is easy to bring the water to a boil, but a good cup of tea takes time and patience; it needs to brew! So it is that each day Jesus warms us with his love and lets it penetrate our whole being. From the treasury of his Sacred Heart, he offers us the grace we need to heal our infirmities and to open our minds and hearts to hear, understand and forgive one another.

We just heard the testimonies of Felicité, Isaac and Ghislain, who are from Burkina Faso. They told us a moving story of forgiveness in the family. The poet says that 'to err is human, to forgive divine'. And that is true: forgiveness is a special gift from God that heals our brokenness and draws us closer to one another and to him. Small and simple acts of forgiveness, renewed each day, are the foundation upon which a solid Christian family life is built. They force us to overcome our pride, our aloofness and embarrassment, and to make peace. How many times do we get angry at one another and then want to make up, but we don't know how! It is embarrassing to make peace, but we still want to do it. It isn't hard. It's easy. Give a caress, and peace is made!

It is true that I like to say that in our families we need to learn three words. Ghislain, you spoke those three words. They

A child watching as Pope Francis makes his way through the crowd, Croke Park, Dublin

Cardinal Kevin Farrell and Pope Francis enjoying the performances on stage, Croke Park, Dublin

are 'sorry', 'please' and 'thank you'. Three words. What were they? Everyone! [all: 'sorry, please, thank you!'] Another time! ['sorry, please, thank you!']. I can't hear you! ['sorry, please, thank you!'] Thank you very much! When you quarrel at home, be sure that before going to bed you apologise and say you are sorry. Before the day is done, make peace. Do you want to know why it is necessary to make peace before ending the day? Because if you don't make peace, the next day you have a 'cold war' and that is very dangerous! Watch out for cold wars in the family! Maybe you get mad sometimes and are tempted to sleep in another room, all by yourself. If you feel that way, just knock on the door and say: 'Please, can I come in?' All it takes is a look, a kiss, a soft word … and everything is back to the way it was! I say this because when families do this, they survive. There is no such thing as a perfect family; without the practice of forgiveness, families can grow sick and gradually collapse.

To 'forgive' means to 'give' something of yourself. Jesus always forgives us. By the power of his forgiveness, we too can forgive others, if we really want to. Isn't that what we pray for, when we say the Our Father? Children learn to forgive when they see their parents forgiving one another. If we understand this, we can appreciate the grandeur of Jesus' teaching about fidelity in marriage. Far from a cold legal obligation, it is above all a powerful promise of God's own fidelity to his word and his unfailing grace. Christ died for us so that we, in turn, might forgive and be reconciled with one another. In this way, as individuals and as families, we can know the truth of Saint Paul's words that, when all else passes away, 'love never ends' (1 Cor 13:8).

Thank you, Nisha and Ted, for your testimony from India, where you are teaching your children how to be a true family. You have helped us to understand that social media is not necessarily a problem for families, but can also

As a good Irish priest taught us, 'the family that prays together, stays together' and radiates peace. In a special way, such a family can be a support for other families that do not live in peace

serve to build a 'web' of friendships, solidarity and mutual support. Families can connect through the internet and draw nourishment from it. Social media can be beneficial if used with moderation and prudence. For example, all of you gathered for this World Meeting of Families have formed a spiritual network, a web of friendship; social media can help you to maintain this connection and expand it to even more families throughout the world. It is important, though, that these media never become a threat to the real web of flesh and blood relationships by imprisoning us in a virtual reality and isolating us from the concrete relationships that challenge us to grow to our full potential in communion with others.

Perhaps Ted and Nisha's story will help all families to question whether they need to cut down on the time they spend with technology, and to spend more quality time with one another and with God. When you use social media too much, you 'spin into orbit'. When at table, instead of talking to one another as a family, everyone starts playing with his or her phone, they 'spin into orbit'. This is dangerous. Why? Because it takes you away from the *concrete reality* of the family and into a life of distraction and unreality. Be careful about this. Remember Ted and Nisha's story; they teach us to make good use of social media.

We have heard from Enass and Sarmaad how a family's love and faith can be a source of strength and peace even amid the violence and destruction caused by war and persecution. Their story reminds us of the tragic situations endured daily by so many families forced to flee their homes in search of security and peace. But they also show us how, starting from the family, and thanks to the solidarity shown by so many other families, lives can be rebuilt and hope born anew. We saw this support in the video of Rammy and his brother Meelad, where Rammy expressed his deep gratitude for the encouragement and help their family received from so many other Christian families worldwide, who made it possible for them to return to their village. In every society, families generate peace, because they teach the virtues of love, acceptance and forgiveness that are the best antidote to the hatred, prejudice and vengeance that can poison the life of individuals and communities.

As a good Irish priest taught us, 'the family that prays together, stays together' and radiates peace. In a special way, such a family can be a support for other families that do not live in peace. Following the death of Father Ganni, Enass, Sarmaad and their family chose forgiveness and reconciliation over hatred and resentment. They saw, in the light of the cross, that evil can only be fought by good, and hatred overcome only by forgiveness. Almost incredibly, they were able to find peace in the love of Christ, a love that makes all things new. This evening they share that peace with us. They prayed. Prayer. Praying together. While I was listening to the choir, I saw a mother teaching her child to make the sign of the cross. Let me ask you, do you teach your children to make the sign of the cross? Yes or no? [all: yes!] Or do you teach them to make some quick wave of the hand [he gestures] that they don't even understand? It is very important that children learn as early as possible to make the sign of the cross *well*. It is the first 'creed' that they learn, a way of saying 'I believe' in the Father, the Son and the Holy Spirit. This evening, before going to bed, ask yourselves, as parents: do I teach my children to make a good sign of the cross? Think about it, it is up to you!

Cardinal Kevin Farrell and Pope Francis enjoying the performances on stage, Croke Park, Dublin

Alison Nevin takes a selfie with Pope Francis, Croke Park, Dublin

The love of Christ that renews all things is what makes marriage and a conjugal love marked by fidelity, indissolubility, unity and openness to life possible. It is what we see in the fourth chapter of *Amoris Laetitia*. We saw this love in Mary and Damian and their family of ten children. Let me ask you [he turns to Mary and Damian], do your children ever make you grow angry? Ah, that is life! But it is beautiful to have ten children. Thank you for your testimony and for your witness of love and faith! You experienced the power of God's love to change your lives completely and to bless you with the joy of a beautiful family. You told us that the key to your family life is truthfulness. From your story, we see how important it is to keep going back to the source of the truth and the love that can change our lives. Who is it? Jesus, who began his public ministry precisely at a wedding feast. There, in Cana, he changed water into a good new wine that kept the joyful celebration going strong.

Did you ever think of what would have happened if Jesus did not perform that miracle? Did you ever think how terrible it would be to finish a wedding feast by drinking just water? It would be awful! Our Lady understood that, and so she told her Son: 'They have no wine.' And Jesus realised that the party would not have ended happily with people just drinking water. Conjugal love is like that. The new wine begins to ferment during the time of engagement, which is necessary but fleeting, and matures throughout marriage in a mutual self-giving that enables spouses to become, from two, 'one flesh'. And also to open their hearts, in turn, to all those in need of love, especially the lonely, the abandoned, the weak and vulnerable so often discarded by our throw-away culture. The culture we are living in today discards everything, everything that is not useful. It discards babies because they are troublesome; it discards the elderly because they aren't useful ... Only love saves us from this throw-away culture.

A society that does not value grandparents is a society that has no future. A Church that is not mindful of the covenant between generations will end up lacking the thing that really matters, which is love

Families everywhere are challenged to keep growing, to keep moving forward, even amid difficulties and limitations, just as past generations did. All of us are part of a great chain of families stretching back to the beginning of time. Our families are a treasury of living memory, as children become parents and grandparents in turn. From them we receive our identity, our values and our faith. We see this in Aldo and Marissa, who have been married for over fifty years. Their marriage is a monument to love and fidelity! Their grandchildren keep them young; their house is filled with laughter, happiness and dancing. It was delightful to see [in the video] the grandmother teaching her granddaughters how to dance! Their love for one another is a gift from God, and it is a gift that they are joyfully passing on to their children and grandchildren.

A society – listen carefully to this! – a society that does not value grandparents is a society that has no future. A Church that is not mindful of the covenant between generations will end up lacking the thing that really matters, which is love. Our grandparents teach us the meaning of conjugal and parental love. They themselves grew up in a family and experienced the love of sons and daughters, brothers and sisters. So they are a treasury of experience, a treasury of wisdom for the new generation. It is a big mistake not to ask the elderly about their experience, or to think that talking to them is a waste of time. Here I would like to thank Missy for her words of witness. She told us that, among travellers, the family has always been a source of strength and solidarity.

Her witness reminds us that, in God's house, there is a place at table for everyone. No one is to be excluded; our love and care must extend to all.

I know it is late and you are tired! So am I! But let me say one last thing to all of you. As families, you are the hope of the Church and of the world! God, Father, Son and Holy Spirit, created mankind in his image and likeness to share in his love, to be a family of families, and to enjoy the peace that he alone can give. By your witness to the Gospel, you can help God's dream to come true. You can help to draw all God's children closer together, so that they can grow in unity and learn what it is for the entire world to live in peace as one great family. For this reason, I wanted to give each of you a copy of *Amoris Laetitia*, prepared in the two synods on the family and written as a kind of roadmap for living joyfully the Gospel of the family. May Mary our Mother, Queen of the Family and Queen of Peace, sustain all of you in your journey of life, love and happiness!

And now, at the conclusion of our evening together, we will recite the prayer for this World Meeting of Families. Let us all recite together the official prayer for the Meeting of Families:

[recitation of the prayer and blessing]

Good night and rest well! See you tomorrow!

By your witness to the Gospel, you can help God's dream to come true

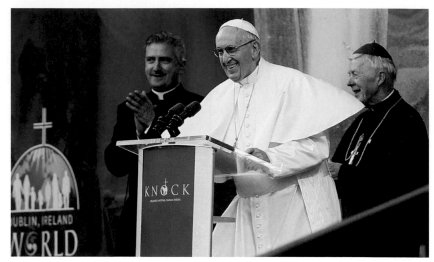

Pope Francis speaking at Knock Shrine

Knock Basilica

Visit to the Knock Shrine

ANGELUS AND POST-ANGELUS GREETING OF HIS HOLINESS POPE FRANCIS

Knock Shrine (Co. Mayo)

Sunday, 26 August 2018

Angelus

Dear brothers and sisters,

I am happy to be here with you. I am happy to be with you in the house of Our Lady. And I thank God for this opportunity, in the context of the World Meeting of Families, to visit this shrine, so dear to the Irish people. I thank Archbishop Neary and the rector, Father Gibbons, for their warm welcome.

In the Apparition Chapel, I lifted up to Our Lady's loving intercession all the families of the world, and, in a special way, your families, the families of Ireland. Mary our Mother knows the joys and struggles felt in each home. Holding them in her Immaculate Heart, she brings them with love to the throne of her Son.

As a remembrance of my visit, I have presented the shrine with a rosary. I know how important the tradition of the family rosary has been in this country. I warmly encourage you to continue this tradition. Who can tell how many hearts, of fathers, mothers and children alike, have drawn comfort and strength over the years from meditating on Our Lady's participation in the joyful, luminous, sorrowful and glorious mysteries of Christ's life!

Pope Francis prays at Knock Shrine

Mary is Mother. Mary is our Mother and the Mother of the Church, and it is to her that we commend today the journey of God's faithful people on this emerald isle. We ask that our families be sustained in their efforts to advance Christ's Kingdom and to care for the least of our brothers and sisters. Amid the storms and winds that buffet our times, may families be a bulwark of faith and goodness, resisting, in the best traditions of this nation, all that would diminish our dignity as men and women created in God's image and called to the sublime destiny of eternal life.

May Our Lady also look with mercy on all the suffering members of her Son's family. In my prayer before her statue, I presented to her in particular all the survivors of abuse committed by members of the Church in Ireland. None of us can fail to be moved by the stories of young people who suffered abuse, were robbed of their innocence, were separated from their mothers, and were left scarred by painful memories. This open wound challenges us to be firm and decisive in the pursuit of truth and justice. I beg the Lord's forgiveness for these sins and for the scandal and betrayal felt by so many others in God's family. I ask our Blessed Mother to intercede for all the survivors of abuse of any kind and to confirm every member of our Christian family in the resolve never again to permit these situations to occur. And to intercede for all of us, so that we can proceed always with justice and remedy, to the extent it depends on us, such violence.

My pilgrimage to Knock also allows me to address a warm greeting to the beloved people of Northern Ireland. Although my journey for the World Meeting of Families does not include a visit to the North, I assure you of my affection and my closeness in prayer. I ask Our Lady to sustain all the members of the Irish family to persevere, as brothers and sisters, in the work of reconciliation. With gratitude for the advance of ecumenism, and the significant growth of friendship and cooperation between the Christian communities, I pray that all Christ's followers will support the continuing efforts to advance the peace process and to build a harmonious and just society for today's children, be they Christians, Muslims, Jews, or of any faith: the children of Ireland.

Now, with these intentions, and all the intentions hidden in our hearts, let us turn to the Blessed Virgin Mary in the prayer of the Angelus.

Post-Angelus Greeting of His Holiness Pope Francis

I offer a special greeting to the men and women in this country who are in prison. I especially thank those who wrote to me upon learning that I would visit Ireland. I would like to say to you: I am close to you, very close. I assure you and your families of my closeness in prayer. May Our Lady of Mercy watch over you and protect you, and strengthen you in faith and hope! Thank you!

Pope Francis with a family at Knock Shrine

Pope Francis arrives at Phoenix Park

World Meeting of Families 2018 Holy Mass

PENITENTIAL ACT, HOMILY AND REMARKS OF HIS HOLINESS POPE FRANCIS

Phoenix Park (Dublin)

Sunday, 26 August 2018

Penitential Act of the Holy Father

Yesterday I met with eight persons who are survivors of the abuse of power, the abuse of conscience and sexual abuse. In reflecting on what they told me, I wish to implore the Lord's mercy for these crimes and to ask forgiveness for them.

We ask forgiveness for the cases of abuse in Ireland, the abuse of power, the abuse of conscience and sexual abuse on the part of representatives of the Church. In a special way, we ask forgiveness for all those abuses that took place in different kinds of institutions directed by men and women religious and other members of the Church. We also ask forgiveness for cases in which many minors were exploited for their labour.

We ask forgiveness for all those times when, as a Church, we did not offer, to the survivors of any type of abuse, compassion and the pursuit of justice and truth by concrete actions. We ask forgiveness.

We ask forgiveness for some members of the hierarchy who took no responsibility for these painful situations and kept silent. We ask forgiveness.

We ask forgiveness for those children who were taken away from their mothers and for all those times when so many single mothers who tried to find their children that had been taken away, or those children who tried to find their mothers, were told that this was a mortal sin. It is not a mortal sin; it is the fourth commandment! We ask forgiveness.

May the Lord preserve and increase this sense of shame and repentance, and grant us the strength to ensure that it never happens again, and that justice is done. Amen.

Homily of His Holiness Pope Francis

'You have the words of eternal life!' (Jn 6:68)

At the end of this World Meeting of Families, we gather as a family around the table of the Lord. We thank God for the many blessings we have received in our families. And we want to commit ourselves to living fully our vocation to be, in the touching words of Saint Thérèse, 'love in the heart of the Church'.

In this precious moment of communion with one another and with the Lord, it is good to pause and consider the source of all the good things we have received. Jesus reveals the origin of these blessings in today's Gospel, when he speaks to his disciples. Many of them were upset, confused or even angry, struggling to accept his 'hard sayings', so contrary to the wisdom of this world. In response, the Lord tells them directly: 'The words I have spoken to you are spirit and life' (Jn 6:63).

> Living in love, even as Christ loved us
> (cf. Eph 5:2), entails imitating his own self-
> sacrifice, dying to ourselves in order to be
> reborn to a greater and more enduring love

These words, with their promise of the gift of the Holy Spirit, are teeming with life for us who accept them in faith. They point to the ultimate source of all the good that we have experienced and celebrated here in these past few days: the Spirit of God, who constantly breathes new life into our world, into our hearts, into our families, into our homes and parishes. Each new day in the life of our families, and each new generation, brings the promise of a new Pentecost, a *domestic Pentecost*, a fresh outpouring of the Spirit, the *Paraclete*, whom Jesus sends as our Advocate, our Consoler and indeed our *Encourager*.

How much our world needs this encouragement that is God's gift and promise! As one of the fruits of this celebration of family life, may you go back to your homes and become a source of encouragement to others, to share with them Jesus' 'words of eternal life'. For your families are both a privileged place for, and an important means of, spreading those words as 'Good News' for everyone, especially those who long to leave behind the desert and the 'house of bondage' (cf. Jos 24:17) for the promised land of hope and freedom.

In today's second reading, Saint Paul tells us that marriage is a sharing in the mystery of Christ's undying fidelity to his bride, the Church (cf. Eph 5:32). Yet this teaching, as magnificent as it is, can appear to some as a 'hard saying'. Because living in love, even as Christ loved us (cf. Eph 5:2), entails imitating his own self-sacrifice, dying to ourselves in order to be reborn

Phoenix Park Mass

Like Saint Columbanus and
his companions, who faced
icy waters and stormy seas to
follow Jesus, may we never be
swayed or discouraged by the
icy stare of indifference or the
stormy winds of hostility

to a greater and more enduring love. The love that alone can save our world from its bondage to sin, selfishness, greed and indifference to the needs of the less fortunate. That is the love we have come to know in Christ Jesus. It became incarnate in our world through a family, and through the witness of Christian families in every age it has the power to break down every barrier in order to reconcile the world to God and to make us what we were always meant to be: a single human family dwelling together in justice, holiness and peace.

The task of bearing witness to this Good News is not easy. Yet the challenges that Christians face today are, in their own way, no less difficult than those faced by the earliest Irish missionaries. I think of Saint Columbanus, who with his small band of companions brought the light of the Gospel to the lands of Europe in an age of darkness and cultural dissolution. Their extraordinary missionary success was not based on tactical methods or strategic plans, no, but on a humble and liberating docility to the promptings of the Holy Spirit. It was their daily witness of fidelity to Christ and to each other that won hearts yearning for a word of grace and helped give birth to the culture of Europe. That witness remains a perennial source of spiritual and missionary renewal for God's holy and faithful people.

Of course, there will always be people who resist the Good News, who 'murmur' at its 'hard words'. Yet like Saint Columbanus and his companions, who faced icy waters and stormy seas to follow Jesus, may we never be swayed or discouraged by the icy stare of indifference or the stormy winds of hostility.

But let us also humbly acknowledge that, if we are honest with ourselves, we too can find the teachings of Jesus hard. How difficult it is always to forgive those who hurt us; how challenging always to welcome the migrant and the stranger; how painful joyfully to bear disappointment, rejection, betrayal; how inconvenient to protect the rights of the most vulnerable, the unborn or the elderly, who seem to impinge upon our own sense of freedom.

Yet it is precisely at those times that the Lord asks us: 'What about you, do you want to go away too?' (Jn 6:67). With the strength of the Spirit to 'encourage' us and with the Lord always at our side, we can answer: 'We believe; we know that you are the Holy One of God' (v. 69). With the people of Israel, we can repeat: 'We too will serve the Lord, for he is our God' (Jos 24:18).

Through the sacraments of Baptism and Confirmation, each Christian is sent forth to be a missionary, 'a missionary disciple' (cf. *Evangelii Gaudium*, 120). The Church as a whole is called to 'go forth' to bring the words of eternal life to all the peripheries of our world. May our celebration today confirm each of you, parents and grandparents, children and young people, men and women, religious brothers and sisters, contemplatives and missionaries, deacons, priests and bishops, to share the joy of the Gospel! Share the Gospel of the family as joy for the world!

As we now prepare to go our separate ways, let us renew our fidelity to the Lord and to the vocation he has given to each of us. Taking up the prayer of Saint Patrick, let each of us repeat with joy: 'Christ within me, Christ behind me, Christ before me, Christ beside me, Christ beneath me, Christ above me' [repeated in Irish]. With the joy and strength given by the Holy Spirit, let us say to him with confidence: 'Lord, to whom shall we go? You have the words of eternal life' (Jn 6:68).

Remarks of His Holiness Pope Francis at the Conclusion of Mass

At the conclusion of this Eucharistic celebration and this marvellous World Meeting of Families, which has been a gift of God to us and to the whole Church, I would like to say a heartfelt 'thank you' to all those who contributed in any way to its realisation. I thank Archbishop Martin and the Archdiocese of Dublin for their work of preparation and organisation, and in a particular way, I express my gratitude for the support and assistance provided by the government, the civil authorities and the many volunteers from Ireland and other countries, who gave so generously of their time and effort. I want to say a special word of thanks to all those who prayed for this Meeting: the elderly, children, men and women religious, the infirm and those in prison ... I am sure that the success of this Meeting is due to their quiet and persevering prayers. Thank you everyone! May the Lord repay you!

Share the Gospel of the family as joy for the world!

Pope Francis arrives at Phoenix Park

Meeting with the Bishops of Ireland

ADDRESS OF THE HOLY FATHER FRANCIS

Convent of the Dominican Sisters (Dublin)

Sunday, 26 August 2018

Dear brother bishops,

As my visit to Ireland comes to a close, I am grateful for this chance to spend a few moments with you. I thank Archbishop Eamon Martin for his gracious words of introduction and I greet all of you with affection in the Lord.

Our meeting tonight takes up the fraternal discussion we shared in Rome last year during your visit *ad Limina Apostolorum*. In these brief remarks, I would like to resume our earlier conversation, in the spirit of the World Meeting of Families we have just celebrated. All of us, as bishops, are conscious of our responsibility to be fathers to God's holy and faithful people. As good fathers, we want to encourage and inspire, to reconcile and unify, and above all, to preserve all the good handed down from generation to generation in this great family which is the Church in Ireland. It is true, the Church in Ireland remains strong; it is true.

So, my word to you this evening is one of encouragement – in line with my homily – for your efforts, in these challenging times, to persevere in your ministry as heralds of the Gospel and shepherds of Christ's flock. In a particular way, I am grateful for the concern you continue to show for the poor, the excluded and those in need of a helping hand, as witnessed most recently by your pastoral letters on the homeless and on substance misuse. I am also grateful for the support you give to your priests, whose hurt and discouragement in the face of recent scandals are often ignored or underestimated. Be close to your priests! For you, as bishops, they are the closest of your neighbours.

A recurrent theme of my visit, of course, has been the Church's need to acknowledge and remedy, with evangelical honesty and courage, past failures – grave sins – with regard to the protection of children and vulnerable adults; among these, women who were mistreated. In recent years, you as a body have resolutely moved forward, not only by undertaking paths of purification and reconciliation with victims and survivors of abuse, but also, with the help of the National Board for Safeguarding Children in the Church in Ireland, you have set in place a stringent set of norms aimed at ensuring the safety of young persons. In these years, all of us have had our eyes opened – painfully – to the gravity and extent of sexual abuse and the abuse of power and conscience in various social settings. In Ireland, as elsewhere, the honesty and integrity with which the Church chooses to confront this painful chapter of her history can offer an example and a warning to society as a whole. Continue on this path. Humiliation is painful, but we have been saved by the humiliation of the Son of God and this gives us courage. The wounds of Christ give us courage. I ask you, please, to be close – this is the word, 'closeness' – to the Lord and to God's people. Closeness. Do not repeat the attitudes of aloofness and clericalism that at times in your history have given the real image of an authoritarian, harsh and autocratic Church.

As we mentioned in our conversation in Rome, the transmission of the faith in its integrity and beauty represents a significant challenge in the context of Ireland's rapidly evolving society. The World Meeting of Families has given us great hope and encouragement that families are growing

With humility and trust in his grace,
may you discern and set out on
new paths for these new times.
Be courageous and creative

more and more conscious of their own irreplaceable role in passing on the faith. Passing on the faith essentially takes place in the family; the faith is passed on in everyday speech, the language of the family. At the same time, Catholic schools and programmes of religious instruction continue to play an indispensable role in creating a culture of faith and a sense of missionary discipleship. I know that this is a source of pastoral concern for all of you. Genuine religious formation calls for faithful and joyful teachers who are able to shape not only minds but also hearts in the love of Christ and in the practice of prayer.

Sometimes we can think that faith formation means teaching religious concepts, and we don't think of forming the heart, shaping attitudes. Yesterday the President of the nation told me that he had written a poem about Descartes and said, more or less: 'The coldness of thought has killed the music of the heart.' Forming the mind, yes, but also the heart. And teaching how to pray: teaching children how to pray from the very start. Prayer. The training of such teachers and the expansion of programmes of adult education are essential for the future of the Christian community, in which a committed laity will be increasingly called to bring the wisdom and values of their faith to their engagement in the varied sectors of the country's social, cultural and political life.

The upheavals of recent years have tested the traditionally strong faith of the Irish people. Yet they have also offered the opportunity for an interior renewal of the Church in this

Phoenix Park Mass

country and pointed to new ways of envisioning its life and mission. 'God is eternal newness' and he impels us 'constantly to set out anew, to pass beyond what is familiar, to the fringes and beyond' (*Gaudete et Exsultate*, 135). With humility and trust in his grace, may you discern and set out on new paths for these new times. Be courageous and creative. Surely, the strong missionary sense rooted in the soul of your people will inspire creative ways of bearing witness to the truth of the Gospel and building up the community of believers in the love of Christ and zeal for the growth of his kingdom.

In your daily efforts to be fathers and shepherds to God's family in this country – fathers, please, and not stepfathers! – may you always be sustained by the hope that trusts in the truth of Christ's words and the certainty of his promises. In every time and place, that truth 'sets free' (Jn 8:32); it has a power all its own to convince minds and draw hearts to itself. Whenever you and your people feel that you are a 'little flock' facing challenges and difficulties, do not grow discouraged. As Saint John of the Cross teaches us, it is in the dark night that the light of faith shines purest in our hearts. And that light will show the way to the renewal of the Christian life in Ireland in the years ahead.

Finally, in the spirit of ecclesial communion, I ask you to continue to foster unity and fraternity among yourselves – this is very important – and, together with the leaders of other Christian communities, to work and pray fervently for reconciliation and peace among all the members of the Irish family. Today, at lunch we were seated, myself, then [the bishops from] Dublin and Northern Ireland ... all together, everyone. There is another thing that I always say, but it bears repeating. What is the first duty of the bishop? I say it to everyone: it is prayer. When the Greek-speaking Christians complained that their widows were being neglected (cf. Acts 6:1), Peter and the apostles created deacons. Then when Peter explained the matter, he concluded by saying: 'We [apostles] will devote ourselves to prayer and to serving the word.' So I throw out a question and each of you can answer it at home: how many hours a day does each of you devote to prayer?

With these thoughts, dear brothers, I assure you of my prayers for your intentions, and I ask you to keep me in your own. To all of you, and to the faithful entrusted to your pastoral care, I impart my blessing as a pledge of joy and strength in our Lord Jesus Christ.

I am close to you: keep moving ahead with courage! The Lord is very good, and Our Lady is watching over you. When things get a little difficult, pray the *Sub tuum praesidium*, because the Russian mystics say that at moments of spiritual turmoil, we should go under the mantle of the Holy Mother of God, *sub tuum praesidium*. Thank you very much! Now I will give you my blessing.

Together let us pray the Hail Mary.

May God bless you all, the Father, the Son and the Holy Spirit.

Thank you very much.

I am close to you: keep moving ahead with courage!